Edited by
ANDREW ROBERTS
NEIL JOHNSON
and **TOM MILTON**

SHARING RESOURCES

66 All the believers
were together and had
everything in common. **99**

The Bible Reading Fellowship
15 The Chambers, Vineyard
Abingdon OX14 3FE
brf.org.uk

The Bible Reading Fellowship (BRF) is a Registered Charity (233280)

ISBN 978 0 85746 682 2
First published 2018
10 9 8 7 6 5 4 3 2 1 0
All rights reserved

Acknowledgements
Unless otherwise acknowledged, scripture quotations from The New Revised Standard
Version of the Bible, Anglicised edition, copyright © 1989, 1995 by the Division of Christian
Education of the National Council of the churches of Christ in the United States of
America. Used by permission. All rights reserved.

Scripture quotations on cover and title page, or marked NIV, are taken from The Holy
Bible, New International Version (Anglicised edition) copyright © 1979, 1984, 2011 by
Biblica. Used by permission of Hodder & Stoughton Publishers, a Hachette UK company.
All rights reserved. 'NIV' is a registered trademark of Biblica. UK trademark number
1448790.

Scripture quotations from the Revised English Bible, copyright © 1989 by Oxford
University Press and Cambridge University Press.

Photograph on page 43 copyright © Thinkstock; photographs on pages 4, 11, 27, 30, 34,
39, 41, 49, 51 and 62 copyright © Tom Milton and the Birmingham Methodist Circuit.

Every effort has been made to trace and contact copyright owners for material used in
this resource. We apologise for any inadvertent omissions or errors, and would ask those
concerned to contact us so that full acknowledgement can be made in the future.

A catalogue record for this book is available from the British Library

Printed and bound by CPI Group (UK) Ltd, Croydon CR0 4YY

CONTENTS

Remember the context

This Holy Habit is set in the context of ten Holy Habits, and the ongoing life of your church and community.

> They devoted themselves to the apostles' teaching and fellowship, to the breaking of bread and the prayers. Awe came upon everyone, because many wonders and signs were being done by the apostles. **All who believed were together and had all things in common**; they would sell their possessions and goods and distribute the proceeds to all, as any had need. Day by day, as they spent much time together in the temple, they broke bread at home and ate their food with glad and generous hearts, praising God and having the goodwill of all the people. And day by day the Lord added to their number those who were being saved.
>
> ACTS 2:42–47

A prayer for the faithful practice of Holy Habits

This prayer starts with a passage from Romans 5:4–5.

> Endurance produces character, and character produces hope,
>   and hope does not disappoint us…
> Gracious and ever-loving God, we offer our lives to you.
> Help us always to be open to your Spirit in our thoughts
>   and feelings and actions.
> Support us as we seek to learn more about those habits of the Christian life
>   which, as we practise them, will form in us the character of Jesus
>   by establishing us in the way of faith, hope and love.
> Amen

INTRODUCTION

In Acts 2:44–45 and 4:32–37, Luke presents pictures of the early Christian communities of disciples supporting one another and those in need in the wider community by the generous sharing of their resources. They shared and sold possessions to create a common fund which could be used to support those in need of income or resources. The fund may also have supported the apostles and, later on, the deacons and others. It was a powerfully prophetic, counter-cultural expression of community then. It remains so today. Much of 21st-century Western culture encourages us to live separate, independent lives protecting our individuality, our privacy and our belongings. The same attitude is also becoming more prominent within the politics of nation states.

In Acts 2:44, we hear that the disciples were together and had 'all things in common'. As you explore this habit of **Sharing Resources**, you may like to reflect on what having all things in common meant to those early Christians, and how we relate that to our lives today personally and collectively in holy living.

This is a particularly challenging habit. It is not about offering others what you can spare. Nor is it about taking from others what you fancy. To share something requires us to change our relationship with that item, perhaps relinquishing our power over it, or taking more account of how we use it. Sharing roles or gifts may mean accepting that a task is not completed to your own exacting standard. Sharing ideas or thoughts may make you vulnerable. True sharing is about working together in an open, honest and thoughtful manner without any hidden agendas. Sharing can be costly and demanding but it is a way to life-giving and transformational experience.

Reflections

I wonder how you would feel if you were sitting in your kitchen, having your first cuppa of the day, and another member of the church let themselves into your home, helped themselves to a cup of sugar, and left again. Or indeed, how comfortable would you feel walking into another church member's home and helping yourself in such a manner? I am sure that we would not begrudge most people a cup of sugar, but I suspect there are very few people we would want to have such free and open access to our private spaces. Similarly, we are very cautious of invading others' privacy.

To have 'all things in common' is about both giving and receiving, and it needs to be mutual. It could mean sharing belongings, skills, ideas, time or roles. **Sharing** may not be the obvious route to take, and it may take courage to initiate it, but from those occasions where we have shared deeply with others, we know that it is often ultimately more rewarding than simply giving.

Sharing Resources involves changing the way we think and the way we operate. As you explore this Holy Habit, think about the different relationships that you have, with individuals, the church, the community and the world. What do you currently have in common and what opportunities are there for sharing and growing that commonality or understanding? You might like to take the 'Share40' challenge outlined later in this booklet. How will your relationships grow and become more exciting by **Sharing** more?

  Resources particularly suitable for children and families

  Resources particularly suitable for young people

CH4 Church Hymnary 4 (also known as Hymns of Glory Songs of Praise)
RS   Rejoice and Sing
SoF Songs of Fellowship 6
StF Singing the Faith

UNDERSTANDING THE HABIT

WORSHIP RESOURCES

Below are some thoughts and ideas for how you might incorporate this Holy Habit into worship.

Biblical material

Old Testament passages:

- Genesis 1:26–31   Humankind is given responsibility for all creation
- 1 Kings 17:1–16   Elijah visits the widow of Zarephath; both give and both receive
- Isaiah 58:6–14   A call to share what we have, to reduce injustice and oppression

Gospel passages:

- Matthew 25:31–46   Sharing what we have is an integral part of following Christ
- Mark 12:41–44   The widow's mite
- Luke 3:7–14   A challenge not to be greedy but to share with those who have not
- Luke 16:1–17   The parable of the shrewd/dishonest manager
- Luke 21:1–4   The widow's mite

Other New Testament passages:

- Acts 4:32—5:16   Sharing in the early church
- Romans 12   New life in Christ leads us to work with each other
- 1 Corinthians 12:1–30   Church is a shared existence in the body of Christ
- 1 Corinthians 13   Sharing without love is nothing
- Galatians 6:1–10   Share each other's burdens
- 2 Peter 1:1–11   Peter calls his readers to be together in mutual affection
- 1 John 3:11–24   The call to love one another

Suggested hymns and songs

- A new commandment I give unto you (RS 745, StF 242)
- A rich young man came seeking (StF 243)
- As we break the bread (RS 439)
- As we gather, Father, seal us (StF 570)
- Because the Saviour prayed that we be one (StF 675)
- Bless and keep us, Lord (RS 471)
- Come, all who look to Christ [God] today (CH4 713, StF 678)
- Community of Christ (StF 681)
- Eternal Ruler of the ceaseless round (CH4 269, RS 623)
- For the fruits of all creation (CH4 231, RS 42, StF 124)
- God in his love for us lent us this planet (RS 85, StF 727)
- In Christ there is no east or west (CH4 624, RS 647, StF 685)
- Jesu, Jesu, fill us with your love (RS 648, StF 249)
- Jesus Christ is waiting (CH4 360, StF 251)
- Let love be real, in giving and receiving (StF 615)
- Now join we, to praise the creator (RS 89)
- One human family God has made (StF 687)
- Put peace into each other's hands (CH4 659, RS 635, StF 712)
- Summoned by the God who made us (StF 689)
- The church is like a table (RS 480)
- The church is wherever God's people are praising (CH4 522, RS 583)
- We are not our own, earth forms us (RS 482)
- We utter our cry (RS 642)

Introduction to the theme 👪

When we think of **Sharing Resources**, it would be easy for our minds to jump instantly to money, possessions and tangible assets. However, 'having all things in common' suggests a much deeper **Sharing** of ourselves and of our lives in the service of God and God's creation.

For this reason, two introductions to the theme are included, to help broaden our understanding of what it means to share our resources.

Share and share alike

Why not let the children share in leading worship? Children understand what it means to share: to share toys, to play together, to learn together. They also know the pain of **Sharing**, as is so often seen in the frequent cry of 'That's mine!'

Ask them beforehand to think about what it means to share, and invite them to write a sketch, poem, song or rap to show the congregation what it means to share. Encourage them to think about what they have enjoyed sharing, and things that they have found difficult to share, and to offer these to God in prayer with the congregation.

Sharing responsibility

What do you value in life? What people, places and moments? We all have moments and places where we get a glimpse of the glory of God through creation around us. For some of us it's found in the work we do, for others it's in the people and places we go to in our free time. In many of our lifetimes, the places where we live have been radically changing and this calls us all to reflect on how we share the world that God has shared with us.

In many places in the world, the reality of human-induced climate change is already being felt. Selina, aged 29, from Bangladesh, takes up the tale.

> Climate change is causing many changes. Previously I used to grow rice, but now this is becoming really difficult. People are beginning to farm fish because the water in the area is so salty, but sometimes it's so salty the fish die. The salt water makes it difficult to grow rice like we used to. It's damaging to our environment and to the rice fields.

Charities like Christian Aid provide ways for individuals and churches to **Share Resources** and to help communities reduce the effects of the changing climate. They challenge governments and businesses to use the resources they have to invest in a more sustainable future. This is because if we share our resources in ways that recognise the interconnected nature of our world, new opportunities can emerge. Storm shelters in the Philippines provided shelter to communities when hurricanes and typhoons hit. As a result of global investment in renewable technology, it is now affordable to put solar panels on the shelters and ensure those sheltering can easily refrigerate any medicines needed.

Sharing Resources to care for creation is a deeply spiritual calling. It challenges us to open our eyes to the world around us. It lifts our eyes beyond our immediate surroundings to take in the enormousness of creation and opens our ears to the voice of the oppressed. By doing so, we are fundamentally challenged and changed. Once we have heard about the reality of a changing climate for people like Selina, we cannot unhear it. We are called to create a more sustainable future.

Thoughts for sermon preparation

Mark 12:41–44

> He sat down opposite the treasury, and watched the crowd putting money into the treasury. Many rich people put in large sums. A poor widow came and put in two small copper coins, which are worth a penny. Then he called his disciples and said to them, 'Truly I tell you, this poor widow has put in more than all those who are contributing to the treasury. For all of them have contributed out of their abundance; but she out of her poverty has put in everything she had, all she had to live on.'

Jesus calls his disciples over to witness the widow offering her last two coins to the treasury. What is it that he wants them to see?

The scriptures consistently instruct that widows, along with foreigners ('aliens') and orphans, should be looked after (see Exodus 22:21–23). The Jews of that time would have been familiar with these responsibilities and yet this woman is allowed to give all that she has to the temple coffers, probably to be used to buy wood and salt for sacrifices, leaving her with nothing. Is Jesus highlighting the hypocrisy of the situation?

Giving of anything – whether money, time or talents – may be sacrificial, but should it be to such an extent that it prevents the giver flourishing? To create a common fund, or any sort of shared resource, each must give according to their means. We have a responsibility to ensure that people are not expected or encouraged to give beyond what they can afford. How often do we allow individuals to give excessively, leaving them with no money, or more often no time, for themselves or for their families?

Alternatively, is Jesus highlighting the need for the widow to give? Both the offering itself, and making the decision to offer, give the widow dignity. Having seen rich people give much, did she feel that she had to give everything to participate – to give less would be too little? To be a community where we hold all things in common, all need to be able to participate and all need to believe that their contributions are valued. Allowing others to contribute fully may mean accepting that things are done differently. It may mean working alongside others to teach them as others taught us, and it may call us to give up our roles, our control or our privilege.

Jesus highlights that the widow shared 'out of her poverty'. In watching her, was he inviting the disciples into that poverty? When we share in another's pain and suffering, or in their lack of resources, are we drawn in? Do we become of one heart? To share with one another should lead us into love, and to love one another should lead us to share. As we share with others, do we grow in love? Does our love drive us to be angry about others' suffering and thus drive us to action to address injustice?

A mother describes how, just days after returning to work after having her second child, her car was stolen. Managing work and nursery drop-offs on public transport would have been challenging. A good friend simply handed over the keys to her car and let her borrow it for a few days until she had found alternative arrangements. This generosity had a profound impact on that mother – how has *our* experience of generosity changed our understanding of **Sharing**?

Sharing is not easy. There are tensions, an inevitable part of being together. They cannot be ignored, but need to be accepted and worked through. Perhaps as we think more about this Holy Habit, we will find that it leads us to become better disciples in ways that may surprise us. Let us encourage one another to think about what each of us has been given by God. How can sharing what we have and who we are, both giving and receiving, be a natural part of our lives – both individually and as a church?

Prayers

A call to worship

Come, whoever you are,
whatever your experience,
whatever it is that defines you.

Come, let us be together,
in one place
and in one time.

Come, let us worship together
as one people,
accepting of our differences
and united in one God.

Come, let us be one with each other and with God.

Come, let us worship together.

A prayer of adoration and confession

When we gather to pray, we pray on behalf of ourselves, the communities we belong to and represent, and the wider world. As you pray this prayer, be conscious of these multiple layers of confession.

Generous God,
you have created a beautiful world for us to live in,
and you have entrusted us to care for it.
You have shared yourself with us,
and invited us to be part of your plan.
You have walked alongside us
and shared our pain and suffering.
You have given us so much.

And yet so often we abuse your trust.
We do not take care of what you have entrusted to us,
and we are unwilling to share fairly with others.

And so, for the times when we have prioritised our need over that of our neighbour,
God forgive us. **Forgive us.**

For the times when others' failings or inadequacies have somehow made us feel better,
God forgive us. **Forgive us.**

For the times when we have not seen the suffering of others,
God forgive us. **Forgive us.**

For the times when we have ignored your role in our lives,
God forgive us. **Forgive us.**

God, help us to remember the source of all that we receive
and to share it more fairly.
Amen

A prayer of intercession

Thank you, Lord, for giving us everything that we have.
Thank you that Jesus remembered those who have nothing,
those who are sitting on the street waiting for something miraculous to happen.
Help us to be like Jesus.
Amen

A prayer when you have lost someone you shared much with

Dear God

We are thankful for loving family and friends.
Together they guide and support us through life.

We pray for those who are not with us and know you are looking after them.
We cherish the memories and good times spent with them.
We know they are in a better place with you.
Amen

A prayer of dismissal

Go in peace,
to give and to receive,
to love and to be loved,
to serve and to be served,
to be united with one another and with Christ.
Amen

Different ways of praying

Finger prayers

Invite people to look at one of their hands.

- Ask them to hold the index finger, and as they do so remember all who point the way for others and think of someone who has pointed the way for them in their life, such as a friend, a family member or a teacher.
- Ask them to hold the middle finger, and as they do so remember all those who are considered important, who hold power and responsibility, and whose decisions affect others, as well as an individual who has particular power over them.
- Ask them to hold the ring finger, and as they do so think of all those who have made commitments and promises to others, as well as someone to whom they have made a commitment or a promise.
- Ask them to hold the little finger, and as they do so remember all those who are considered unimportant, as well as someone they know experiencing weakness, frailty or vulnerability.
- Ask them to hold the thumb, and as they do so give thanks for Jesus who makes it possible for the fingers to work together. Offer a prayer for the **Sharing of Resources** so that all of the gifts God has given might be used for the building of community, and the coming of God's kingdom in peace, love and justice.

End by creating a chain of hands (if using cutouts) or linking hands in a circle, and then raise them in blessing for the world and all its people.

Finish by praying the following prayer:

Gracious God,
we thank you for all that you have given us,
the people, the places, our daily bread and our hopes and dreams.
Thank you for all your good gifts.
Amen

Offering

Instead of doing a monetary collection one week, why not take up an offering of gifts, talents or roles that people are willing to take on or support? This is an opportunity for people to offer unknown talents or passions, or to volunteer for things that they would be willing to take on in the life of the church. These could be written on small cards and received during the service. It might be helpful to warn people in advance that this will happen so they can reflect on and pray about how to respond.

God of abundance,
You have given each of us different gifts, talents and passions.
We offer all these to you for your kingdom.
Encourage and guide us as we work together
so that we may all use what we have been given
to further your work here on earth.
In Jesus' name.
Amen

A focus for personal prayer

Give each member of the congregation a small piece of card and a pen. Invite them to discuss in twos and threes what is on their hearts and minds. You might need to practise this kind of sharing until people feel confident that they can safely share themselves and their burdens with honesty and openness.

Ask each person to write or draw on their piece of card one or two things they have just heard that have stirred them. Ask them to take the card home and commit to praying regularly for the things on it during the following week.

Dove of peace: prayers for others

Each person will need a paper dove and a pen.

Share with those gathered that many of us are extremely privileged, as we live in countries that know peace. Acknowledge that some of those gathered may have lived in countries or in times where there has been political unrest or war. Others will have experienced or be experiencing a lack of internal peace, either personally or in the lives of those they love.

Ask everyone to hold their dove and think of people or places about which they are concerned. Invite them to write the name of or draw the person, place or situation that comes to mind, on the dove. As they write or draw, encourage them to ask God to send peace and love to that person, place or situation.

Invite the congregation to pin the doves to a piece of hanging fabric, to a 'washing line' or to a notice board as a communal act of prayer. This could be done in silence or with music playing in the background or, if it is a service of Holy Communion, as people come up to receive.

Testimony

Could you introduce a regular slot into your **Worship** where people are invited to share experiences with the whole congregation, or in twos or threes? Starting with a simple, accessible example, such as a beautiful sight, might encourage more people to engage in future weeks.

You could move on to answer one of these questions: 'Where have you noticed that God has been present in your life this week?'; 'Have you had any prayers that have been answered this week?'.

Alternatively, you might like to consider another question relevant to the service or liturgical season.

GROUP MATERIAL AND ACTIVITIES

Some of these small group materials are traditional Bible studies, some are more diverse session plans and others are short activities, reflections and discussions. Please choose materials appropriate to whatever group you are working with.

Sharing in the early church

Acts 4:32—5:16

There is a lot of material in this session, which may be better spread over several meetings.

Background

The call to the adventure of Christian discipleship that we are exploring from the characteristics of the early church described in Acts 2:42–47 is echoed in particular ways in this later passage. In between, Luke has described a sequence of events around the temple. Peter and John heal a man lame from birth. Peter responds to the amazement of the crowd in a bold proclamation of the gospel. The authorities perceive this as provocation and Peter and John are arrested, but many believe. A description follows of the trial and the gathering of believers to which Peter and John report after they are set free. Under threat, they respond in confidence, seeking strength to continue to proclaim the good news of Jesus and to bring healing and other signs and wonders.

Much of the book of Acts is about the church looking outward, travelling on, bringing healing and confronting the status quo – sometimes making friends, at other times facing opposition. However, occasionally the focus changes and we are invited to look inwards; this passage is one such interlude where the reader is encouraged to think about what it means to be one holy community: in the words of the NIV, 'All the believers were one in heart and mind' (Acts 4:32). Some will see this passage as historical reality; others will view it as an idealised and theologically profound portrait of what a community of faith could be.

Prayer

As you gather for prayer, encourage the group to look around and be aware of the resources we share together as we meet. There may be comfortable furnishings, hospitality and refreshments, different versions of the Bible, a prayer book or concordance.

There is a cost to some of these things. Perhaps the greater cost is what we risk when we are willing to share of ourselves. Invite the group to think about the less tangible things we share as we meet together (e.g. ideas, experiences, values, stories, silence, understandings, fellowship).

- Are we willing to share our knowledge, to be open about our doubts and uncertainties, to share our understanding of the biblical text and to share stories from our experiences?
- How willing are we to give space to others, to hear what they bring?
- Are we willing to sacrifice our own opinions and the opportunity to speak, in order to encourage others to grow in faith?

Bring these thoughts together in prayer:
Sharing God, Father, Son and Spirit,
We rest in the quiet, thankful for your presence with us as we meet.

(*Silence*)

Speak to us through your word,
in the voices of others
and in the silence speak into our thoughts.

(*Silence*)

Bless us with your Spirit,
enter into our hearts and minds
as we share together with one another
that we may know you better
and go away equipped to share your love with others.
Amen

Reading and discussion

Share the text by reading it aloud and then give space for each person to read it to themselves to see if a word or phrase strikes them. Allow sufficient time for this, remembering that some people need time to savour things for a while before being ready to share.

Invite people to contribute their word or phrase, and to say how it made them feel – e.g. curious to know more, cheered, concerned, energised or depressed. Sometimes people find it helpful to unpack their response in some detail. This could take the whole of your allotted time, and may well be a way in which you come to notice God's promptings. On other occasions, it may take only a few moments, in which case the following questions may be helpful.

1 What does the group make of verse 32, 'one in heart and mind' (NIV) or 'of one heart and soul' (NRSV), and the concept of sharing everything they had? Is this possible, desirable or necessary for a community to be Christ-following? Are there circumstances where this could be helpful or where it could be dangerous?
2 Verse 32 is followed by a reminder of the power of the community and the writer is prompted to return to the resurrection of Christ. What might the links be between verses 32 and 33? God's grace is given before any faith or response – might we prefer verse 33 to come before 32? Might this make a difference to our thinking about question 1?
3 How do we, both as individuals and as church communities, relate to verse 34, 'there was not a needy person among them'?

After the introductory section, there are two specific examples of sharing: encouragement in the case of Barnabas and a warning in the case of Ananias and Sapphira.

1 Barnabas, we are told, is a Levite (a group dedicated to Israel's spiritual wellbeing rather than stewards of the promised land – Deuteronomy 12:12; Joshua 14:3–4). He comes from Cyprus, not from Israel. At Pentecost, when the Jews of the diaspora (the word used to describe the Jews that lived outside Jerusalem) return to Jerusalem and share understanding, he is given a new name by the apostles as someone who is a man of encouragement, or as one whom others are encouraged to imitate. What might have enabled him to share so profusely? Are there individuals or groups whom we see as Barnabas?
2 Responding to God's grace does not always make us as generous and life-giving as Barnabas, so with heavy hearts we turn to the story of Ananias and Sapphira. Notice what Ananias does and doesn't do: he is generous, he gives some of his wealth, but he doesn't tell the truth and his gift turns from being life-giving to

being death-dealing. There are all sorts of reasons why Ananias and Sapphira might have held back; it might be helpful to consider some of them to work out when and how we find it easy to be generous and when and how we find the need to hold back. Why might they not have given everything? Have another look at verses 3–4. Do you think Peter is angry, perplexed, sorrowful, disappointed or just furious? Ask yourselves the same question about verse 9.

3 What are we to make of the deaths? Are they to be understood as punishment, coincidence or an illustration of how deception and holding back from generosity bring suffering and diminish all those involved?

Application

The Pentecost experience in Acts 2 was one of profound **Sharing**. As 'Pentecost people', our sharing in the resurrection life given by the Spirit brings mutual understanding, and is a key part of our discipleship.

- What encouragement for **Sharing Resources**, both spiritual and material, can Barnabas give us?
- How might this be life-giving for ourselves, for our church, for our community?
- What warnings about the fear of **Sharing Resources** and of speaking the truth can Ananias and Sapphira give us?
- How might this speak to us, to our church, to our community?
- How do we feel when people ask for volunteers at church, work or home?
- How might each of us continue to develop the Holy Habit of **Sharing Resources** this week?

Closing prayer

Perhaps you could use some of your conversation from the application section to offer a prayer of blessing for one another, giving thanks for the resources of time, thinking and conversation you have shared as well as your commitment to share with those you will meet in the coming days.

Spend a moment of quiet reflecting on how this session will feed into your prayers.

Further reflection

For a follow-up session, consider the final sentence under 'Background' (p. 21). Think about how those in your group see the passage and whether this matters or not.

Mine or ours? ☺

Ask people to write down a list of their possessions, and then another list of shared possessions in their households. Be aware that this activity could make some feel uncomfortable. Make it clear that you are not necessarily talking about expensive items. You could give a 60-second time limit for each list.

Discuss how people feel about sharing the shared possessions. Then discuss how they feel about sharing their own possessions. Encourage the group to look back through their list and to arrange it into an order from those possessions that they would least want to share to those that they would be happy to share. Discuss whether they think that people care too much about their possessions – why might this be? Do they think it is bad to own too many possessions?

Either read the first three paragraphs from Ian Mead below, or ask one person to read them out.

> I live as a member of a Benedictine community. There are 13 of us who worship, work, and live together.
>
> Of course, sharing material resources makes sense in many ways on a practical level. For example, we don't need 13 lots of kitchen appliances or garden tools; we can share together in the work that needs to be done and in the resources that we have. There is also one common fund and any income any of us receives is put in that fund and is used to purchase what is needed for the community.
>
> Sometimes, however, this can be difficult; maybe I can't do a particular job now because someone else is using the equipment, or I need to compromise my own desires and wants in a particular area to allow for the needs of the other members of the community.
>
> These practical issues point to something deeper. What does it mean to be a member of the body of Christ? Sharing things together helps me to realise that my discipleship is not a solo journey. I am walking a path with others and as I share with them I meet Christ. Am I open to that blessing?

Ask people how Ian's life differs from theirs, and whether his lifestyle seems attractive or unattractive – and why.

If you are exploring this session with young people, you may want to discuss with them when they think they might share their possessions differently in the future, for example in student houses or future partnerships. With older people, you may want to discuss when they have shared possessions differently at different stages of their lives.

Explain that the early church did not live as a monastic community. The believers still had their own possessions, but they would make them available to others if they were needed. If we recognise that everything we have belongs to God, rather than to us, does that make it any easier to share our possessions? (Remember that sharing doesn't necessarily mean giving away.)

Ask what people find helpful and challenging about the way the early church approached ownership. You may want to explore this question as a discussion, or you may prefer to give each person a small square of card to write on one side what they find helpful, on the other side the challenges, and then to use that card as a focus for their prayers.

You may want to finish the session with a challenge to the group to look for opportunities to share their possessions with others who need them, and then to feed back on their experiences over the coming weeks.

Different gifts 👪

1 Corinthians 12:27–30

Take four volunteers and sit them down facing the rest of the group.

1. Blindfold one person, play music through earphones for the second to wear (just loud enough to prevent them from hearing the instructions clearly), tie the third person's hands behind their back and do nothing to the fourth.
2. Place a piece of paper and a pen in front of each of the volunteers.
3. Ask them to draw a dog.

The first three people will probably draw to varying levels of success, but only the one with all their limbs and senses will be able to draw a reasonable dog.

Read 1 Corinthians 12:27–30. Sitting in a circle, ask people to draw around their hand on a piece of paper and write their name in the middle. Then pass this to the

person on their left. They then have to write a gift or talent which the original person has. Continue to do this until everybody has written something in each hand.

Reread 1 Corinthians 27–30.

Explain how we all have different gifts. First, think of different gifts within the church. There is a preacher who understands the Bible and can share that understanding with others. There are pastoral visitors who have the gift to help others. There are those blessed with the gift of working with young people and so they do. If the preachers refuse to work with the pastoral workers, what happens if someone hears the message in church and wants someone to talk to? Or if one of the pastoral visitors has visited someone who is upset and needs someone to talk about the Bible with them? Each of us has a different gift; it is our duty to work together so that the church can reach people in all situations.

Now think how you share your gifts in everyday life as part of your discipleship at work, at school or college, at home, in the community, in the issues of the world and campaigns for justice.

- How do you share your gifts?
- With whom do you share your gifts?
- How might the church support you as you share your gifts with others?

Many heads are better than one: sharing wins! 👪

Give each member of the group a small pile of sticky notes of one colour. Ask them to think of fun ideas for an evening for the group, and to write each on a separate sticky note. They should do this in silence and not let each other see what they are writing. When the allotted time is up, collect in all the spare sticky notes, and record on a flipchart how many ideas each person has had.

Now give out sticky notes of a different colour, before inviting the group to share the notes that they have already written and stick each on a board or wall. As this is happening, encourage them to write down new ideas that occur to them.

At the end of the activity, count the total number of ideas that have been generated in the original colour of sticky notes and in the second colour. Show the group how the total number of ideas generated from the group was greater than the number from any one person, highlighting how many extra ideas were generated when they started sharing their ideas together.

Explain that studying the Bible may also be better done collectively than on your own. Invite people to take a passage that is appropriate for their context and maturity (e.g. a creation story, Joshua and the walls of Jericho, Jonah). Read the passage together and invite everybody to note down the questions that the passage raises for them. When they have done this, help them to use the discussion of their questions to explore the passage together.

Sharing through playing games

Try playing Monopoly with the normal rules, except that each time an unowned property is landed on, all the players have the opportunity to buy it together as a shared resource (meaning that any rent collected is shared among all of the owners). Reflect on how this simple change makes the game a very different experience. How does this change the way we think about the world?

There are a number of games available that help players to understand more about how the world's resources are shared, often unfairly. One such game is the Trading Game (**learn.christianaid.org.uk/YouthLeaderResources/trading_game.aspx**). Play this game to show how trade affects the prosperity of a country – both positively and negatively.

Sharing food 👪 ☺

Using food or cooking together can be a good way to explore what it means to share our resources and talents. One example could be to cook pizza together. Ask a couple of people to make the dough, others to make the tomato sauce and others the toppings. Then all share the results together.

Another example could be to invite each person to bring a random ingredient from home, and to spend the session using the different ingredients to create a meal.

Vulnerability and sharing

Many churches share their buildings with other groups. There is always an element of risk involved in doing this. What are the implications in relation to Holy Habits for those hosting diverse groups as they respond to the challenge to share God's mission? A complex range of issues and relationships is evident. It is essential to develop good relationships and build trust, and to ensure good communication and effective consultation. Clarity is needed on both sides of the relationship about expectations and the need for continual re-assessment should be recognised.

The version of the great commission in Luke 24:45–49 might be seen as a model for relating to the people who use 'our' church premises. These are the ones that are 'in Jerusalem' and it is where we can start our mission, by being witnesses to the faith. It raises questions about our relationship with those who use our premises.

- How do we regard these groups?
- How do we relate to them?
- What sort of relationship should we have?
- How do we build relationships?
- How do we support users in their work, assuming that we believe that they are contributing to the life of the community?
- How is our service to them 'distinctively Christian'?
- What is the evidence that it is 'loving'?
- What criteria and conditions do we have in place for renting out our building?
- Are there groups whose use of our premises makes us feel vulnerable?
- How can we ensure that contracts reflect the spirit of generosity?
- How do we respond when (inevitably) there are complaints by the users or about the users?
- How do we witness to the faith and the life of faith?

Shared drawings 👪

Give each person a piece of paper. Invite them to draw a hat at the top of the page in the middle. Then ask them to fold the top of the page over backwards so that all but the very base (1 mm) of the hat is hidden from them and the remaining blank part of that side of the paper is to the front.

Pass the pieces of paper around and invite each person to draw a head and neck connecting to the base of the hat that they cannot see and then again to fold it over backwards so only the bottom 1 mm is visible.

Passing the papers around after each section, draw the upper body, then the lower body and finally the feet. The papers should then be passed around one last time.

Each person unfolds their sheet revealing a full person created by them together. Show the group how working together they have been more creative than they could have been alone.

Start a discussion about how this relates to the way in which you **Share Resources** personally and in your church.

FORMING THE HABIT

The ideas presented in this section are offered to help you establish or further practise **Sharing Resources** as a regular habit personally, as a church and in engagement with your local community and the wider world. You may want to consider using the ideas in more than one of these contexts.

In developing **Sharing Resources** as a regular habit, you may find some of the material in the 'Understanding the habit' section helpful too.

STORIES TO SHOW THE HABIT FORMING

How could you use these formative and transformative stories to inspire others? What stories of your own could you share? There are many ways in which Christians can **Share Resources** and many types of resource that can be shared, including the greatest resource of all: love.

In Andrew Roberts' book, *Holy Habits* (Malcolm Down Publishing, 2016), he shares the story of Allan and Lyn:

> Allan and Lyn are model givers of love. Having raised their own three children, they became foster parents. Their modest Black Country home became a sanctuary of love, peace and healing to a succession of children. From babes in arms to those nearing school age, many of them had experienced very difficult starts in life. Whenever I called round, there seemed to be a new child being blessed with the gift of a loving home amidst the joyous chaos of bottles and buggies, Telly Tubbies and toddler tantrums.

On the Fresh Expressions website (**community.sharetheguide.org/views/joining-the-marginalised**), Jennie Appleby shares some challenging thoughts from her time serving in a small northern town where she deliberately chose to live in an area that no estate agent would dare call 'desirable'. She says:

> Life amongst this new community was transformative and there was never a dull moment. Frequent sights of furniture being moved between houses (usually on foot), early morning police raids and unconventional offers of cheap electrical items were everyday occurrences. I realised I'd been accepted in the community when I was invited by two women to join them for a drink at the local working men's club, and when someone turned up on my doorstep to ask for prayer.

> Amidst the colourful lives on the estate and the disbelief of Christians from the other side of town, I discovered a sense of the tangible presence of God. I could imagine Jesus himself walking the streets with me and I experienced signs of God's kingdom: people sharing their lives and possessions together – not out of a sense of Christian love or duty but because they had so little themselves. I had never witnessed people sharing on this level before – they were teaching me lessons about how to live the Christian life.

The Inn Churches project in Bradford (**www.innchurches.co.uk**) coordinates churches across the city in opening their doors to homeless people for a week each over the winter months. Guests are referred by a wide range of agencies and are welcomed with a hot dinner each night, a warm bed and a good breakfast. More than just a sharing of food and buildings, though, members of the churches sit alongside the guests and get to know them, sharing their time. In addition, Inn Churches works with the guests to support them into longer term accommodation.

In a story that has now been written up in many places, possibly originating in Jim Wallis' book *On God's Side: What religion forgets and politics hasn't learned about serving the common good* (Brazos Press, 2013), Heartsong Methodist Church shared their resources with their new Muslim neighbours:

> A group of Muslims bought a piece of land next to Heartsong Methodist Church in Memphis, Tennessee, to build a mosque and community centre. The church thought hard about how to react. They put up a big notice outside telling their Muslim neighbours that they were welcome. The Muslims were so surprised and pleased they went to talk to the minister, who asked what his church could do to help them. They asked if they could rent a little room as temporary accommodation – he let them have the biggest room they had. When they had a church barbecue, they bought halal meat so they could invite the Muslims. They began to work together on neighbourhood projects to help the poor.

> A journalist from CNN alleged that they never published good news stories about Muslims because there aren't any. Someone challenged them to report what was happening at Heartsong, so they made a 90-second video about the church, which was looped on the CNN news channel over the course of a day. A few days later, the minister had a phone call from Kashmir. The caller said that he and his friends had been sitting in a café watching CNN when the story about the Muslims and the Christians came on. They were speechless when they saw it because they had been told that all Americans hated Muslims. They did not think Christians could get on with Muslims. They talked about what they could do in response to what they had seen of the Methodists at Heartsong and they decided that they should take care of the little Christian church in their community. They went and cleaned the church inside and out, washing off the offensive graffiti which had been daubed there. They made the minister a promise that, for the rest of their lives, they would take care of the Christians in their community as the people at Heartsong had taken care of their Muslim neighbours.

A Christian leaving university got a job with a major car manufacturer. Naturally, he soon owned a car. Some friends of his had two young children but could not afford a car of their own. The man with the car added his friends to his insurance so that they could use the car to go on holiday. They, in turn, opened their home to their friend, who was single, sharing with him meals and the fun of a family home. A simple, practical (and economically efficient!) sharing of resources. Might you do something similar?

Deborah Humphries, a minister in the Birmingham Methodist Circuit, writes:

> As part of my university language studies, I spent two months in the L'Arche community at Trosly-Breuil. In the daily routine of living alongside people with and without learning disabilities, eating, praying, cleaning, singing, caring for one another and sharing life together, I learned much about sharing and what it means to live in community. Living alongside people who were unable to communicate verbally, I discovered the beauty of sharing at a deep and spiritual level where a look or a sound often said so much more than words. In this profoundly peaceful place where life was not always easy, but where joy and pain were expressed freely and openly shared, I caught more than a glimpse of the kingdom of God – a depth of sharing which lives with me and continues to sustain me to this day.

The Bradford Central food bank operates as many Trussell Trust food banks do, providing emergency food to those referred to the service. However, one of the striking things has been how many of the former clients are now involved in volunteering with and supporting the food bank, wanting to share the love and care that was given to them when they needed it most with others who are now in need.

PRACTICES TO HELP FORM THE HABIT

Here are some suggestions for how **Sharing Resources** can be part of a rhythm or rule of life in our personal discipleship and in and through the **Fellowship** of our churches.

To share or not to share

There may be people in your congregation who have autism, dementia or mental health issues, who find it difficult to share but who want to be part of the church. Each person will have different needs and it is important that we embrace these. Have you spoken to them (or, where it is more appropriate, to their carer) about how you can enable them to participate and share more in the life of the church? In time, they might feel able to share with the congregation about their particular situation and so increase everyone's understanding.

Sharing in this way should never be about sharing for sharing's sake; rather, it should be about building God's kingdom as we learn to share with those who might experience life differently from ourselves.

As lives and experiences are shared and as understanding grows and develops, so the kingdom will be more fully known and realised.

Sharing which is honest and open can make us vulnerable, and although being vulnerable is not bad in itself, we must always ensure that appropriate safeguards are in place.

Often (daily or weekly)

> ## Journalling
>
> Journalling is regularly reflecting on your experiences, thoughts and encounters with God and keeping a note of your reflections. See the Holy Habits Introductory Guide for more information.
>
> Record in your journal opportunities you have had to share your resources. Note down the different emotions or attitudes connected to these occasions. When have you found it easy to share? When have you found it difficult? Has your attitude towards your own possessions changed in any way? Reflect on what you have done to make this a habit and how it has been affecting your discipleship.

Share your gifts and skills

Are there opportunities to work with other local churches, perhaps **Sharing Resources** or skills to enable something to happen that would not be viable in a single church? For example, could you form an ecumenical youth club?

Share yourself

How often do we truthfully answer the question, 'How are you?' Or how often do we ask it without really wanting to hear more than the briefest of answers?

Michael Forster's hymn, 'Let love be real', has much to challenge us about how we share ourselves. As we develop the Holy Habit of **Sharing Resources**, might we be able to grow our churches and communities so that they become safe places where weaknesses can be honestly shared and pretence is absent? As we share of ourselves, might we journey towards wholeness, recognising and accepting that we are not yet fully complete?

Share community

Sharing stories of suffering leads to understanding and action. Organisations such as CitizensUK (**www.citizensuk.org**) help different community organisations to listen effectively and to work together, to give the voiceless a voice and enable communities to tackle issues. Could you get involved in a local chapter of CitizensUK, or an organisation in your area bringing communities together?

Share the joys and pains of the world

What response do you habitually have to the events in the news? Do you turn away, or give of yourself to make it better? How could this be more of a positive habit for you and your church?

To reflect on this more fully, you may wish to listen to the song 'Don't dream it's over' by Crowded House, or the hymn 'Have you heard God's voice' by Jacqueline Jones, both of which explore contrasting responses to the news.

Share your spending power

Our buying choices can influence how the world's resources are distributed. The choice of where we spend our money determines whether we support practices such as slavery, exploitation and plundering of natural resources – or whether we support a fair distribution of wealth, organic and sustainable farming and a living wage.

One significant way in which we can **Share Resources** to make positive kingdom difference is to embrace, practise and campaign for fair trade.

Fair trade
There are various fair trade organisations under the umbrella of the Fairtrade Foundation, all with the aim of supporting farmers, workers and artisans in the developing world to trade their way out of poverty. As a result, approximately 165 million people in over 74 countries are being helped.

The main Christian fair trade organisation is Traidcraft, which operates in churches and shops throughout the UK. Traidcraft has three main areas of work:

- Trade: sourcing products from the most marginalised groups in developing countries, often working with suppliers that mainstream businesses choose not to work with and who may not produce goods in sufficient quantities to obtain the Fairtrade logo
- Development work: giving people the skills, knowledge and support they need to lift themselves out of poverty, e.g. empowering people, especially women, to work collectively
- Campaigning: lobbying governments and working with businesses and institutions to deliver policies that ensure a fairer deal for people in developing countries.

Paying a fairer price for goods does mean that items are often a little more expensive then the non-fairly traded ones. But trading fairly enables individual producers to afford life's essentials such as education and healthcare, and whole communities to benefit from the Fairtrade premium with, for example, the provision of clean water supplies.

For more information, go to **www.fairtrade.org.uk** or **www.traidcraft.co.uk**.

Do you look for the fair trade alternatives? Could you become a Fairtrade church?

Campaigning

Consider **Sharing Resources** of time, knowledge and advocacy by campaigning on an issue of local, national or international justice. Use the resources of voice and freedom of speech to speak up on behalf of those who are denied their freedom.

Financial giving

This material is adapted from Andrew Roberts, *Holy Habits* (Malcolm Down Publishing, 2016), pp. 166–68.

Often, when it comes to the sharing of resources or giving, we immediately think of money. As this booklet makes clear, there are many resources we can share, but it would be remiss not to encourage reflection on the practices of financial giving, both of churches and of individual disciples. As you explore this Holy Habit, you may well wish to reflect upon this aspect of **Sharing Resources**.

For many disciples today, the practices of tithes and offerings as outlined in the Hebrew scriptures continue to inform and guide their giving of resources (Leviticus 27:30–32; Deuteronomy 14:22–29). This is still common practice in many churches. There is no doubt these practices release resources that are conducive to the growth and mission of Christian communities.

In the West Midlands, a new church was planted in the hall of a school. Within two years, a community of around 30 were meeting regularly and employed their own pastor. Some other local Christians looked on in a mix of awe, wonder and envy. 'How can you do that?' they asked. 'Because we tithe,' came the succinct answer.

At this point it is important to note that, while the practice of tithing is not rescinded in the New Testament, it is not specifically endorsed by Jesus, Paul or anyone else. This may be of course because it was simply accepted as a given – a continuation of Jewish practices.

Jesus talks about money more than any other subject, but he never does so in a legalistic, percentage-based prescriptive way. Rather, he uses stories and examples to point people to the divine impulse of generous giving. Perhaps the most moving and challenging story about giving is that often called 'The widow's mite'.

> [Jesus] looked up and saw rich people putting their gifts into the treasury; he also saw a poor widow put in two small copper coins. He said, "Truly I tell you, this poor widow has put in more than all of them; for all of them have contributed out of their abundance, but she out of her poverty has put in all she had to live on.
>
> LUKE 21:1–4

The sacrificial generosity of the widow is stunning but by no means unique. So often it is those who have the least financially or materially who are most generous with their giving. Simon Guillebaud tells a story like those told by many receiving hospitality in homes of families that are materially poor but spiritually rich.

> I've been overwhelmed by the sacrificial sharing of destitute believers in Burundi. I drove to a displacement camp. They had no electricity, water or sanitation. After the church service, I was taken to a tin shack, and fed beans and rice. I knew this was far beyond what they could afford. They were giving me so much out of their little, as so often we give so little out of so much.
>
> Simon Guillebaud, *More Than Conquerors* (Monarch Books, 2009), pp. 142–43

There are no percentages, rules or prescriptions here, just extravagant generosity of kingdom proportions.

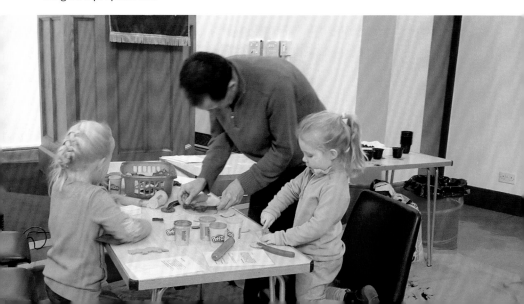

Share resources in your community

Could you set up a toy, jigsaw or game library with the local community?

Could you share your skills and gifts with the community by hosting a craft fair or talent competition in the church?

Share your building

Have your church building or grounds got features that could be valuable to your community? Could the local community be invited to share them for a one-off occasion or a more permanent arrangement as part of your missional life?

For example, could you allow the local Job Centre Plus to hold a jobs fair on the premises, or could you create a community prayer garden? One church in Stoke-on-Trent housed the local library when council cutbacks meant that a dedicated library building could no longer be provided. Other churches have hosted post offices.

Be generous with your **Sharing**. Do you make your buildings available to others but lock up all the teaspoons behind stern notices? Consider how to make users feel welcome by clearly labelling things and making things easy to use. If certain items do need to be reserved, make sure your explanations or notices are kindly worded.

Share, don't hoard

Invite people to reflect on their possessions. For those who have an abundance, how might they be encouraged to live more simply and to share their surplus with others? Could people be invited to sell goods on eBay and to share the money raised to support those with very little? Or could they donate goods to charity shops so that charities can benefit from the sharing of these resources?

Share creation

Encourage people to think bigger and beyond possessions. How might you share a local resource of pathways and parks in God-honouring, other-people-serving ways? Might you adopt a patch of land to keep tidy or do some 'guerrilla gardening', planting flowers to brighten up the neighbourhood?

How might you welcome newcomers to the area, including refugees and asylum seekers, sharing your home, your church, your community with them?

How could you modify your lifestyle, energy usage and buying choices to share more equitably the resources of the earth?

Plan a season of sharing

To develop this Holy Habit and to make it part of the natural rhythm of the life of your church, why not plan a season of sharing with simple ideas and activities that encourage and enable people to **Share Resources** personally, locally and globally? Advent, with its focus on giving, and Lent, with its focus on discipline and self-denial, would both be good times to do this. A different season could be the school summer holidays when you share the resources of your church to support children, families and older people for whom regular services are often reduced at this time of year.

A range of resources are available to support such seasons. This is particularly true of Lent, where the Church House Publishing resource *Love Life Live Lent* is particularly popular.

You could also produce your own programme, as the Birmingham Methodist Circuit did with their 'Share40' programme (**www.birminghammethodistcircuit.org. uk/news/why-not-try-to-share40-things-this-lent**), which sets the challenge to complete 40 sharing activities during a fixed time. These include having lunch with a friend, watching a film with someone, praying with someone, buying Fairtrade products and sharing a recipe.

Develop a rule or rhythm of life

Could you develop a rule or rhythm of life which includes practical commitments to living simply and generously, with resources seen as gifts not possessions?

Rhythms of life can be very simple. The Hebrew prophet Micah provides a famous early example:

> What does the Lord require of you but to do justice, and to love kindness, and to walk humbly with your God?
> MICAH 6:8

Alternatively, they can be more sophisticated and nuanced to the ethos of a particular group of disciples. The VentureFX pioneers, an evolving missional community within the Methodist Church, has adopted the following rhythm of life:

We are committed to a rhythm of life which flows from three core values:

- ○ Innovation: breaking new ground and planting for the future
- ○ Imagination: dreaming God's vision for what church could become
- ○ Incarnation: immersed in our communities in the name of Christ.

We seek to express those values by:

- ○ daily reflecting on our spiritual journey as disciples of Jesus
- ○ weekly observing a common day for the discipline of prayer and fasting
- ○ monthly gathering together for support, encouragement and learning
- ○ annually sharing in a retreat to renew our individual and common life with God.

(See www.methodist.org.uk/media/636034/venturefx-rhythm-of-life-0912.pdf.)

There is a wealth of helpful writings and resources around rhythms and rules of life, for example:

- Ian Adams, *Cave Refectory Road* (Canterbury Press Norwich, 2010), chapter 6
- Ian Mobsby and Mark Berry, *A New Monastic Handbook: From vision to practice* (Canterbury Press Norwich, 2014), chapters 4–5
- Robert Wicks, *Everyday Simplicity: A practical guide to spiritual growth* (Ave Maria Press, 2000)
- Contemplative Fire's rhythm of life at **community.sharetheguide.org/stories/contemplativefire**
- **www.methodist.org.uk/media/831306/dd-explore-devotion-writing-a-rule-of-life-0313.pdf**.
- Simon Reed, *Followers of the Way* (BRF, 2017).

QUESTIONS TO CONSIDER AS A CHURCH

These questions will help your church to consider how it can review the place of **Sharing Resources** in all of its life together. They are intended to be asked regularly rather than considered once and then forgotten. You will need to determine where in your church the responsibility for each question lies – with the whole church in a general meeting, or with the church leadership, a relevant committee or another grouping. Feel free to add more of your own.

- The believers were all together and had 'all things in common'. How does your church (denominationally and locally) understand this phrase? Some thoughts from denominations and organisations are included later in this booklet. Might you organise a series of services or home groups to unpack and explore this phrase?
- What do you have in common with your community? How might you **Share Resources** with the local community and around the world?
- How can those in need, within the fellowship and beyond, share their needs without embarrassment?
- Could you develop a rule of life as a church?
- What does your church budget reveal about your attitudes to **Sharing Resources**?
- What attitudes might need challenging – for example, a comment made by one church member, 'They're not having any of *my* money'? To what extent are the resources of followers of Jesus 'mine'?

- Financial giving is not the only way we share our resources, but it has always been an important aspect of Christian discipleship. How might you encourage people and the church collectively to review their practices of giving?
- Do you encourage everyone to use their gifts and skills for the kingdom or do a few people dominate and restrict others taking part, either intentionally or subconsciously? Whose resources willingly offered might be ignored?
- How could you have more things in common with those who share their resources on a daily basis as a practical outworking of love, for example foster carers, those caring for relatives or new parents?
- Do we share the church's resources well within the church community? Do children and young people have the same access to resources as adults in the church?

CONNECTING THE HABITS

PRAYER

Sharing your time in **Prayer** can be very powerful, and particularly helpful at times when personal prayer is difficult.

BREAKING BREAD

When **Breaking Bread** together as a church, why not then take bread to neighbours or strangers and give it as a gift to them, with a prayer that Christ would be encountered in the gift?

WORSHIP

The word *liturgy* means 'the work of the people'. How might **Worship** utilise the gifted resources of all the people who gather?

GLADNESS AND GENEROSITY

Gladness and Generosity turn what might otherwise be a duty into a delight.

SHARING RESOURCES IS A HOLY HABIT AS OLD AS CREATION, WHEN GOD CREATED AN INTERDEPENDENT UNIVERSE

How might meals you eat be shared with those in need or who are otherwise not part of the church, or who cannot attend services regularly?

EATING TOGETHER

The shared 'community of goods' in Acts modelled kingdom living and gave practical expression to **Fellowship**. How might your church mirror this?

FELLOWSHIP

Shared stories of Jesus at work in people's lives are often an integral part of discipleship journeys. The witness of a community that truly gives to anyone who is in need, or uses their gifts and talents selflessly to meet the needs of the wider world, is highly attractive in **Making More Disciples**.

Consider the economic models that **Biblical Teaching** encourages and the implications of these.

SERVING

MAKING MORE DISCIPLES

BIBLICAL TEACHING

GOING FURTHER WITH THE HABIT

DEVELOPING FURTHER PRACTICES OF SHARING RESOURCES

The meaning of Christ's solidarity with humanity

There is an activity in the **Serving** booklet on Matthew 25:31–46 (the parable of the sheep and the goats). Here are some further thoughts on how that passage relates to **Sharing Resources**, as well as to the understanding of *koinonia* in the **Fellowship** booklet.

The doctrine of the Incarnation tells us that, in Jesus, God took on the form of a particular human being who lived at a particular time in a particular place. But the New Testament tells us also that Jesus became *the* representative human being, standing for the whole human race, just as in Genesis 2—3 Adam represents the whole human race. So, in 1 Corinthians 15:22, Paul can say, 'As all die in Adam, so all will be made alive in Christ.' Throughout his letters, Paul constantly refers to us being 'in Christ', and in more than one place he also speaks of us being 'members' of Christ's body – not in the modern sense of membership of an institution, but in the original sense of a member as part of a body. Just as the eternal Son of God was manifested in the body of Jesus, so after the resurrection and ascension the Son of God is present in what is now the body of Christ, and in its 'members'. As Paul says in the Revised English Bible translation of 1 Corinthians 12:27, 'Now you are Christ's body, and each of you a limb or organ of it.'

Mother Teresa took this a step further when she spoke of 'seeing and adoring the presence of Jesus, especially… in the distressing disguise of the poor' (*In the Heart of the World: Thoughts, stories and prayers*, New World Library, 1997). In saying this, she brings us directly into contact with the meaning of Matthew 25:31–46. The parable calls us to serve others and to **Share Resources** with them, but behind this lies a bigger and deeper mystery, in the sense in which Paul uses the word, for example in Ephesians 3:4. This is the mystery of Christ who is now present in his body in this world, 'and each of [us] a limb or organ of it'. So it is that Jesus tells those on his right hand in the parable that what they have done to the least of his brothers and sisters they have done to him.

As you practise the holy habit of **Sharing Resources**, you may wish to reflect on how you are encountering and sharing Jesus in so doing.

All things in common

'All things in common' is a striking phrase at the heart of the Holy Habits passage (Acts 2:42–47). It powerfully encapsulates the practical outworking of the deep relationships (*koinonia* – **Fellowship**) that were a prophetic hallmark of the kingdom way of living modelled by the church that Luke describes. Throughout church history, different groups and communities of Christians have interpreted and modelled this way of being in different ways. Some, especially monastic communities, have interpreted this in a very disciplined way.

Here are a few thoughts on how some denominations and traditions seek to live out having 'all things in common'. If you are part of a different tradition, you might want to explore what it says about this way of living.

The Methodist Church seeks to be Christian community by living as a 'Connexion'. Rachel Lampard, 2016/17 Vice-President of the Methodist Conference, explains:

> Connexionalism isn't just a way of organising ourselves; rather, it is a way of being Christian. We are all parts of the body and together we make up the whole. We are connected to one another through the love and grace of Jesus Christ. We are diverse but interdependent. Joined together, we form the whole. As a Connexion, we believe that no local church – or minister – can be an autonomous unit complete in themselves. We all contribute and we all receive.

> But we're not a random selection of things tied together. So, secondly, we share self-similarity: each part of us has the same characteristics as the whole. What are the characteristics we all share? Put simply, it's God's love. Look at each of us individually – we see God's love reflected there. Look at each church – we see God's love. Look at the Methodist Church in Britain, or in the world – we see God's love. The self-similarity in our Connexion is the love of God. And thirdly, the whole is incomplete without any one part of it. There is no hierarchy of importance within the church; the newest and freshest growth is as important and vital as every other component. It is incomplete without every part; the church is incomplete without you.

John Proctor, General Secretary of the United Reformed Church, writes:

Every Christian is part of a big family, reaching around the world. 'Sisters and brothers', the Bible calls us – one family in the fellowship of Jesus Christ.

Your local church is the place where that family meets your life. As Christians, we belong together, depend on one another and grow through sharing in work and worship. We know Christ better when we see his light reflected in other people's lives. Local church makes that experience real.

Yet local church is only one fragment of a much larger family. As the United Reformed Church, with over 1,000 congregations across Scotland, Wales and England, we aim to serve and support one another as one body in Christ.

We care too about wider links. So we build the best contact we can with churches of other traditions, labels or styles. Especially if our church buildings stand close to one another, we want to work together, and offer a shared witness to our local community.

The URC values international connections, and has strong bonds with churches from all around the world. We learn from them, share with them and grow through knowing them.

Finally, we belong with the church of the past and the future: people who loved Jesus before we were born, who brought the faith to our land and to our generation; and people yet unborn, who will love Jesus in times to come. We are family, one family in Jesus.

David Cornick, General Secretary of Churches Together in England, adds:

The body of Christ worldwide is composed of literally hundreds of separate denominations – one of the sad consequences of the schism between East and West in 1054, compounded by the divisions of Latin Christendom following the reformations of the 16th century. Thanks to migration and the movement of peoples over the last century or so, the world church is now on Britain's high streets, so those divisions are profoundly in our midst.

As we all read our Lord's prayer in John's Gospel, that his followers might be one, we know the plethora of splits is wrong, and that in God's good intent we belong to each other. Whether we be Orthodox, Catholic, Protestant, charismatic or evangelical, we know we are bound together as fellow Christians by bonds that we do not yet understand, for God's ways are not ours. However, our age is characterised by a remarkable ability to share in varied traditions of prayer and spirituality. We sing each other's hymns, learn from each other's saints and holy ones, immerse ourselves in each other's praise. That is a rich gift.

We are also learning to recognise each other's integrities and limitations, and to be patient with each other. Beliefs about who may be a priest or a bishop, about who may preside or receive at the Eucharist, or who may speak at a council of the church are never intended to constrict or constrain fellow believers of different traditions, but to express profoundly held beliefs about what the church is and how in Christ it ought to be ordered. The long and painstaking ecumenical task is to enter into each other's spiritualities in such a way that we can appreciate those differences from a point of view other than our own.

That is uncomfortable because its takes us out of our comfort zone. But when we have the courage to do it, we discover ourselves growing deeper into the totality of Christ, for he is both the head of the church, and the Word through whom all things were made and are reconciled. We need to make that spiritual journey, for as we make it we will discover anew the riches of God's resources which are there to sustain us on our earthly pilgrimage.

As you reflect on these thoughts on 'all things in common', ask yourself:

- How do you experience oneness in Christ between churches in your location?
- How could the unity Jesus prayed for be more fully realised and expressed in your context?

Holy Habits and political resistance

URC Mission Enabler Kevin Snyman shares some reflections on how challenging it can sometimes be to share our resources.

I spent some time among the Occupy Londoners in 2011/12 and, surprisingly, learned something about the early church of Luke and Acts. There were fascinating parallels, in spite of the vast differences between these disparate communities.

Both situations arose as a direct consequence of the debilitating effects of empire – Roman back then, and military-corporate-economic today. In both contexts, the poor bore the burden of insanely unequal wealth distribution.

Jesus enabled those most affected by the systems of the 'World' to realise a different 'kingdom': a programme of repentance from collusion with empire, resistance to its seductions, refusal to use its methods and a radical new God-way of living. This included abundance over scarcity, sharing over hoarding, caring over self-centredness, giving over taking, grace over law and an unwavering commitment to the most vulnerable.

In Occupy, one could catch a glimpse of the kinds of community envisioned in Acts: dispersed authority, direct democracy, refusal to be co-opted by power, sharing of food and tents, free university, free toilet facilities and a shared desire for a better world.

St Paul's Cathedral was in a desperate place: if they showed solidarity with the tent-dwellers, whose cries for justice could no doubt be heard by the tentmaker himself, they risked the ire of their wealthy benefactors. But not to help would be a terrible, reputational risk. They desperately sought a middle way. Sadly, once Giles Fraser (former Canon Chancellor of St Paul's) left, they buckled under the pressure, chose to close their doors (for the first time since World War II), generally refused to offer toilet facilities or food and finally agreed for the police to evict the protesters. I often wonder what Jesus made of these actions.

Sharing your story

Are there people within your church or wider community who can share stories of how **Sharing Resources** has changed their life (verbally, visually or in written form)? There may be people who have received from others in time of need; or perhaps more interestingly there may be people who have volunteered believing they were sharing themselves, their time, money or resources, only to find that they themselves have been the recipients of others' sharing.

Find stories of local projects which encourage sharing in its widest sense and challenge members of the congregation to 'have a go' and then report back (e.g. hearing children read, car sharing, listening to people who are housebound).

Within a safe space, perhaps in small groups, invite people to share how they have been challenged by the Holy Habit of **Sharing Resources**, to share where they think they have been changed and where they might still need to change.

ARTS AND MEDIA

There are many films and books containing scenes about **Sharing Resources** which could be used as an illustration in worship. However, it is suggested that the following films and books are watched or read in their entirety and followed by a discussion to go deeper into the topic of **Sharing Resources**.

Films

The Blind Side (12A, 2009, 2h9m)

A true story about a homeless and traumatised teenager who has drifted in and out of the school system. He is taken in by a caring woman and her family. As a result, his life turns around, despite setbacks, and he achieves success as a professional American football player.

- How can we share the resources of our homes with others?

 **Despicable Me** (U, 2010, 1h35m)

Comedy in which Gru, a grumpy evil mastermind, hatches a plan to steal a shrink-ray from another evil genius. Gru adopts three orphans in order to gain access to the shrink-ray, but unfortunately (or fortunately) for him, this doesn't go to plan. His three new adopted daughters turn his life upside down and their love for their new dad rapidly shifts his priorities.

- How does sharing his life with the orphans transform Gru's life?
- Can you share your own **Sharing Resources** transformation stories with one another?

Groundhog Day (PG, 1993, 1h41m)

A man finds himself living the same day over and over again on repeat. At first, he uses this discovery for his own personal gain, but in time, he learns there is very little to be gained in this and turns his hand to sharing and making things better for others.

- Are there moments or days you would like to relive so that you could share more?
- If you had to relive the past day, how and with whom would you share more?

Hotel for Dogs (U, 2009, 1h40m)

A story about two teenagers who move into the home of their new guardians, who forbid them to get a pet. However, after finding a stray dog, the pair decide to start a new project to home stray animals. Others in the community get involved and share their money and soon, despite their own tough situation, the teenagers are running a successful project.

- Sharing the abandoned hotel with dogs brings a new lease of life to a disused building and changes the lives of those involved. How can **Sharing Resources** in your setting bring about transformation and change?

I, Daniel Blake (15, 2016, 1h40m)

A British drama in which a 59-year-old joiner, unable to work due to a recent heart attack, befriends a young single mother as they both struggle with the red tape of the British benefits system. In an Amos-style world, a small Acts-style community fights back.

- How does this film challenge our beliefs and/or prejudices about the benefits system?
- How can we share what we have learnt?

Pay It Forward (12, 2000, 2h3m)

A film about a young boy who receives a kindness and decides to share it by passing on a kindness to someone else. This grows into a movement called 'pay it forward'.

- How can receiving from others (and from God) make us different?

Books: fiction

Are there people in your church or local community who would like to discuss some of these books at a book club? Guidance on how to form these is widely available online, and you could also ask denominational training officers for help.

A Hunger Artist
Franz Kafka (originally published in *Die neue Rundschau*, 1922)

This short story eerily and hauntingly depicts human depravity in its fascination with, and pleasure in, the suffering of fellow human beings. If we don't do anything about injustice and inequity, then we are not only depraved spectators but willing actors in communal social criminality. **Sharing Resources** is a Christian tenet we must grasp urgently if we are to stop being collectively 'entertained' by the suffering of others.

- How should we respond to depictions of suffering?
- How can we resist the temptation to turn off, turn over or walk on by?

Charlotte's Web
E.B. White (Harper & Brothers, 1952)

This book is the story of a friendship between a pig and a spider. The animals in the barn **Share Resources**: Charlotte shares her life-saving web-writing skills and receives a meal from the flies that buzz round the others; Wilbur shares his food with Templeton, the rat who goes to look for 'new words' for Charlotte. The message of new life and hope with Charlotte's children at the end also fits a death and resurrection theme for Easter. Adapted into a film of the same name (U, 2006, 1h37m).

- Discuss the change that happens on the farm because of the different ways in which the characters share. Can you see any parallels between life on the farm and life in your church and community?

Lila
Marilynne Robinson (Farrar, Straus & Giroux, 2014)

In this novel (the third instalment of the Gilead trilogy), Lila shows herself to be incredibly generous with her very limited material possessions, but finds sharing her experiences and feelings much more difficult.

- What do we find difficult to share and why?
- How might we get better at sharing those things?

Pumpkin Soup
Helen Cooper (Corgi, 1999)

Three animals, Cat, Duck and Squirrel, live together in the old white cabin, each doing their special job.

- Is this true sharing?
- What happens when the status quo is challenged?
- How could you practise more generously the kind of sharing encouraged by the story?

Squirrel's Busy Day
Lucy Barnard (QED Publishing, 2013)

A book about a squirrel who is too busy to speak to his friends because he is collecting nuts in his little trailer. Then he spills all of his nuts and is stuck! But his friends rally round and help him to get the nuts back in the trailer so he will be secure for winter.

- How easy is it to let others help or share with us?
- How important is it to share our time with others?
- How is asking for help a way of **Sharing Resources**?

Still Alice
Lisa Genova (Wheeler Publishing, 2007)

This novel gives an insight into living with dementia and how easy it is for sufferers to feel excluded.

- What could we do in our churches and in our communities to reduce or prevent this happening?

Books: non-fiction

Beatrice: The Cadbury heiress who gave away her fortune
Fiona Joseph (Foxwell Press, 2012)

A biography of Beatrice Cadbury (1884–1976), heiress of the world-famous chocolate empire. Beatrice discovers that being wealthy in a world of people who don't have very much isn't all that it's cracked up to be. She decides to give away all her shares in the company and what happens next isn't what she might have expected.

- Are you called to give away or share 'your' resources?
- To what extent are 'your' resources yours?

Jesus and Money: A guide for times of financial crisis
Ben Witherington III (SPCK, 2010)

Jesus spoke about money more than any other subject. For better or worse, money influences the way that most resources are shared. Here is a scholarly work that examines how Jesus' teaching can shape the way we think about money.

- When did you last review your practices of financial giving as an aspect of your discipleship? If not recently, spend some time reviewing those practices.

Boundaries: When to say yes, how to say no, to take control of your life
Henry Cloud and John Townsend (revised edition, Zondervan, 2002)

A sharing of wisdom about boundaries – when to say yes? When to say no? What are good boundaries? Where do they come from? How can we make good boundaries? Grounded in Christian thought, this book helps the reader to think through and learn more about creating healthy boundaries. **Sharing Resources** is not meant to deplete us and make us ill, but to be a healthy, positive thing for all involved. This book will help any reader in ensuring it is so.

- How can we be happy with what we are giving and receiving in work, home life, church and relationships?

Christianity, Climate Change and Sustainable Living
Nick Spencer and Robert White (SPCK, 2007)

An analysis of the scientific, sociological, economic and theological thinking that makes a Christian response to unsustainable patterns of consumption and production in the West and explores what Christians, church fellowships and the church can do and campaign about.

- What might your church do to encourage sustainable practices?
- How might you respond to the impact of environmental degradation locally and globally?

For further reading on climate change, consider reading the *Encyclical on Climate Change and Inequality* by Pope Francis and Naomi Oreskes (Melville House, 2015).

Dethroning Mammon: Making money serve grace
Justin Welby (Bloomsbury Continuum, 2016)

This is a very accessible book that can be read by oneself or in a group. Money is an important resource. What does it mean to dethrone Mammon in the values and priorities of our civilisation and in our own existence? As we learn to trust in the abundance and grace of God, anything might and probably will happen. Be prepared for a thought-provoking journey with decision and action.

- How do we handle the power of money?
- Which kingdom values are particularly important for shaping your economic thinking and practices?

Rejection, Resistance and Resurrection: Speaking out on racism in the church
Mukti Barton (Darton Longman & Todd, 2005)

The many painful experiences described in this book highlight how churches can exclude those who are not 'like us'.

- How do you feel about the stories in this book?
- Are there similar stories in your community?
- How can you ensure that **Sharing Resources** happens inclusively in your church and community?

Tuesdays with Morrie
Mitch Albom (Doubleday, 1997, new edition 2007)

The writer goes to visit an old professor and realises he is lonely and ill. He goes to visit regularly, thinking he is doing a good thing, but realises over time that he is gaining so much from listening to Morrie's wisdom and life-lessons. When we share our resources (such as time or energy), we sometimes find we receive more than we give. Sometimes **Sharing Resources** ends up giving us huge resources back in a different way.

- Talk with your pastoral visitors about how far this book resonates with their experience of visiting others.

Articles and online media

Good News Stories

Baxter Job Club and FoodBank (**youtu.be/wF60wCMpHw4** or search YouTube for 'Good News Stories with Nick'). This story is also listed in **Gladness and Generosity** and **Serving**.

Regenerate and Repair (**youtu.be/AbqjqLr0aPg** or search YouTube for 'Good News Stories with Nick'). This story is also listed in **Serving**.

Radical Hospitality

'Kind is…' (**youtu.be/jT-nhBVxrqA**, or search YouTube for 'Kind is… Radical Hospitality') shows that small things which we might take for granted can make a huge difference to those who have to go without.

Music

The following songs may help you to explore and reflect further on this habit.

Do they know it's Christmas?
Band Aid

Take time to reflect upon this song and what it says about attitudes to **Sharing Resources** and how they might have changed since this song was written.

The Sharing Song
Jack Johnson

Poetry

A number of poems are referenced below. Choose one to reflect on.

You may wish to consider some of the following questions:

- What does this poem say to you about **Sharing Resources**?
- Which images do you find helpful or unhelpful?
- How is your practice of **Sharing Resources** challenged by this poem?
- Could you write a poem to share with others the virtues of **Sharing Resources**?

Unfurlings 9: The Well of Goodness
Ian Adams, from *Unfurling* (Canterbury Press, 2015)

Gift
R.S. Thomas, from *Collected Poems 1945–1990* (Phoenix Giant, 1993)

Watching a Documentary about Polar Bears Trying to Survive on the Melting Ice Floes
Mary Oliver, from *Red Bird* (Bloodaxe Books, 2008)

The Son of Man is Come

Ralph Beyer (1921–2008): pencil, 1961, 20 x 38 cm.
From the Methodist Modern Art Collection, © TMCP, used with permission.
You can download this image from: www.methodist.org.uk/artcollection

This is a study for one of the 'Tablets of the Word' at Coventry Cathedral. There are eight tablets (large stone blocks) carrying carved texts and symbols placed around the nave walls of the new cathedral. The cathedral's architect, Sir Basil Spence, commissioned this study from Beyer, who came to England as a refugee from Nazi Germany in 1937. 'The Good Shepherd', with the sheep on the shepherd's shoulders, is a symbol found in early Christian sculpture and in inscriptions on the Roman catacombs. These inscriptions had a profound influence on the style of lettering adopted by Beyer, who developed a career as a freelance sculptor and teacher of lettering.

- The context for Beyer's work was the devastation and sacrifice of World War II. How would you link this with his choice of biblical texts (Luke 19:10; John 10:11)?
- Take a look also at Isaiah 40:11 and Ezekiel 34:2–31. What characteristics form that of the good shepherd, according to the Old Testament prophets?
- What are the largest personal sacrifices you have been called upon to make?

Occupy

Explore the contradictions in this photo of the 'Occupy' camp outside St Paul's Cathedral in London in October 2011. In what ways might **Sharing Resources** as a Holy Habit be countercultural and even controversial?

Credits

In addition to the Holy Habits editorial/development team, contributions to this booklet also came from: Tina Brooker, John Cooper, Brian Dickens, Caroline Homan, Linda Innes, Vincent Jambawo, Leverne Johnson, Rachel Lampard, Becca Lees, Andrew Mason, Ian Mead, Sarah Middleton, Tom Milton, Amy Oliver, Fiona Rees, Marjorie Roper and Cleopas Sibanda.

'This set of ten resources will enable churches and individuals to begin to establish "habits of faithfulness". In the United Reformed Church, we are calling this process of developing discipleship, "Walking the Way: Living the life of Jesus today" and I have no doubt that this comprehensive set of resources will enable us to do just that.'
Revd Richard Church, Deputy General Secretary (Discipleship), United Reformed Church

'Here are some varied and rich resources to help further deepen our discipleship of Christ, encouraging and enabling us to adopt the life-transforming habits that make for following Jesus.'
Revd Dr Martyn Atkins, Team Leader & Superintendent Minister, Methodist Central Hall, Westminster

'The Holy Habits resources will help you, your church, your fellowship group, to engage in a journey of discovery about what it really means to be a disciple today. I know you will be encouraged, challenged and inspired as you read and work your way through each chapter. There is lots to study together and pray about, and that can only be good as our churches today seek to bring about the kingdom of God.'
Revd Loraine Mellor, President of the Methodist Conference 2017/18

'The Holy Habits resources help weave the spiritual through everyday life. They're a great tool that just get better with use. They help us grow in our desire to follow Jesus as their concern is formation not simply information.'
Olive Fleming Drane and John Drane

'The Holy Habits resources are an insightful and comprehensive manual for living in the way of Jesus in the 21st century: an imaginative, faithful and practical gift for the church that will sustain and invigorate our life and mission in a demanding world. The Holy Habits resources are potentially transformational for a church.'
Revd Ian Adams, Mission Spirituality Adviser for Church Mission Society

'To understand the disciplines of the Christian life without practising them habitually is like owning a fine collection of soap but never having a wash. The team behind Holy Habits knows this, which is why they have produced these excellent and practical resources. Use them, and by God's grace you will grow in holiness.'
Paul Bayes, Bishop of Liverpool

'The Holy Habits resources are a rich mine of activities for all ages to help change minds, attitudes and behaviours. I love the way many different people groups are represented and celebrated, and the constant references to the complex realities of 21st-century life.'
Lucy Moore, Founder of BRF's Messy Church